Copyright © 2017 Patrick Hoeller

Publisher: tredition, Hamburg, Germany

ISBN
Paperback: 978-3-7323-8560-7
Hardcover: 978-3-7323-8561-4
eBook: 978-3-7323-8562-1

Printed on demand in many countries

Let it all go

Patrick Hoeller

LET IT ALL GO

PATRICK HOELLER

Sometimes you need to stop analysing the past, stop planning the future, stop figuring out precisely how you feel, stop deciding exactly what you want, and start trusting the process, believing in timing, going with the flow and just see what happens. Knowing yourself is the process of understanding what human being you are on a deeper level. It is an unpredictable road that you must be willing to explore. It brings you face to face with your deep self-doubts and insecurities.

It makes you take a serious look at the way you are living your life. It will take a while, but in the end it will all be worth it because of the abundance that will be showered from the universe. Knowing yourself means respecting your values in life, your beliefs, personality, priorities, moods, habits, and getting to know your body and your personal relationships. Knowing yourself means understanding your desires and dreams. Knowing your life purpose to fulfil before returning back home.

If you can't do anything about it, then let it go.

Don't be a prisoner to things you cannot change.

0: Introduction

Have you ever wondered how your life would have turned out if you hadn't walked down the path you are on at present? Have you ever noticed after all you went through, the rollercoaster moments experienced and been on, the anxiety and depression kicked in and felt, the sleepless nights, vivid experiences lived, that all you ever wanted and wished for became reality eventually in the strangest but also surprising ways at the right time?

Have you ever imagined one day you would wake up and feel the freshness and lightness within your heart, the freedom and love within yourself? That is the moment you have come back home, returned to the start, closed chapters that needed to be left behind, learned important lessons presented on a silver plate to become a better version of yourself, and experience pure and clean love from within. Decide to trust the process, but mostly see the clear vision at the end of the tunnel. All you ever needed to do was to let it all go.

No one said it would be easy and no one would have taken a step or walked a mile in your shoes, but looking back you have realised life has a funny way of working things out exactly at the right time, not a second before or after. What you gave out in this process of personal growth you got back in return in the most magical ways. The soul has been set free and living in the moment was essential to find the peace you had been looking for so long in others around you, when it was always there in you.

This life has been given to you for a reason, and you might have discovered that. But have you also fully understood the strength that comes from within, and that happiness will only be found in your true self? Let it all go, as only then you will be able to start from where the puzzle has been left in pieces, from a place where you once thought you were fully complete but discovered there is so much more in you as a human being, who has touched ground once again to live the life you were chosen to live.

Re-born and newly created as a whole. When you let go, you forgive. When you forgive you won't change the past, but you will change your own future. Be an example; work hard and be yourself. Do your thing and believe that you create your own reality. Pick yourself up and smile a little bit more, hold your head up and express what you have learned on your journey. Give love as you want to be loved, and feel emotions as they come. If you want something you have never had, then you have to do something you have never done. You only have one shot; make it count.

No matter what you have lost or how you were hurt, there is no future for you in your painful hurt, there is no future for you in your painful memories. The past may have given you awareness, but it is not awareness. The past is real, but it is as ephemeral, as unreal and as unreachable as any other illusion. Memories are illusions, echoes of the past. They are a form of false consciousness, a place one lives to avoid living.

As your past emerges in your mind, you vanish in the present. If you are not careful, your memories can imprison you. Stop thinking about what you wish to repair from the past. You cannot heal memories; you can only heal yourself in the present. All your pain from the past has already served you. Keep the lessons of your pain, but not the memories of it. Let it all go.

Chapter 1: The past, the present and the future

Yesterday is gone. Tomorrow has not yet come. The past is a ghost, the future a dream; all you ever have is now. Yesterday is history, tomorrow a mystery. Today is a gift, which is why you call it the present. You have only today. The past and future are real illusions; they exist in the present. Gratitude looks to the past and love to the present. Fear, avarice, lust and ambition look ahead. In life there is only the present moment, the now. You cannot measure time the way you measure the distance between two points. Time does not pass.

You, as a human being, always think about what you did, how you could have done it better, and the consequences of your actions or why you did not act as you should have. All you think about is the future; what you are going to do tomorrow, what precautions you should take, what danger awaits you around the corner, how to get what you have always dreamt of or how to avoid what you do not want.

You are constantly being told, when in depression, that your judgement is compromised. But there is a part of depression that touches cognition. Having a breakdown does not mean that your life is a mess. If there are issues you have successfully skirted or avoided for years, they come cropping back up and stare you full in the face. One aspect of depression is a deep knowledge that the comforting doctors who assure you that your judgement is bad are wrong. You are in touch with the real terribleness of your life.

You can accept that rationally later, after the medication sets in; you will be better able to deal with the terribleness, but you will not be free of it. When you are depressed, the past and future are absorbed entirely by the present moment, as in the world of a three year old child. You cannot remember a time when you felt better, or at least not clearly, and you certainly cannot imagine a future when you will feel better. There is the past and there is the future.

The present is never more than the single second dividing one from the other. You live poised on that second as it hurtles forward - towards what? Even when you lost everything you thought there was to lose, somebody came along and gave you something for free. The present defines the future. The future builds on the foundation of the past. It is being here now that is important. There is no past and there is no future. Time is a very misleading thing. All there ever is is the present. You can gain experience from the past, but you cannot relive it; you can hope for the future, but you do not know if there is one.

You have to try to say something different in the future, something you haven't said before. If you want to fly in the sky, you need to leave the earth. If you want to move forward, you need to let go of the past that drags you down. There are times in our lives when you have to realise your past is precisely what it is and you cannot change it. But you can change the story you tell yourself and by doing that, you can change the future, learn from your mistakes and move forward, hoping for change. There is an open road full of wonder waiting for you. The magic is letting it all go.

Chapter 2: Knowing who you are

The older you get, the more you understand how your conscience works. Amazing, magical things happen when you stop seeking approval and validation. That will be the moment you find it, find who you are and what you are here for. People will naturally be drawn like magnets to you, those who know who they are and cannot be shaken, without limiting themselves to their own expectations of who they are. When you know from within, you do not need to know further. When you know the mediator within, you do not need to mediate further.

When you truly know your own journey, the one inside you, you are ready to be led. By fixing your attention almost instantly on the facts actually before you, you may force them to turn into adventures, force them to give up their meaning and fulfil your mysterious purpose. No one else knows what you went through or are still going through - shifts in your life, emotions, feelings, struggles, highs or lows. Only you do. If you know who you are from within, your ego will get a feeling of security. You will feel safe instead of fearful, and in no time you will open up to explore.

It is important, not for your ego but for your soul, to know that you have been the best even though deep inside you know you will never be better than that. Knowing who you are also defines other important things, no matter how hard life presses at you. One of those things is that wherever you are, and no matter for how long, there must be a home to hold you. You cannot know who you are unless you are contained in some way that gives you shape. Otherwise you are like a puff of wind or water disappearing in the sand. You have no way of knowing if you will be there in a day or a week.

You must let your destiny come to you. In one sense this is always true. Each of you need to be defined to live, not just wait to live. Living in the present, knowing yourself, and who you are. Socrates beautifully phrased it, "To know yourself is the beginning of wisdom". What exactly do you know when you know yourself? As you live your daily life, you can look for clues to this important self-building. Why is it important to know yourself? A little secrecy is a great pillar of the mind. He who does not have what somebody does not know, has what everybody knows.

Know your secret. Keep your secret. He who knows what to keep knows what real life is all about. Knowing why you are is your purpose, knowing who you are is your style and knowing what you are is your character. When you know who you truly are, the need to compare yourself to others becomes completely unnecessary. The first benefit of self-knowledge is happiness. You will be happier when you express who you are. Your desires, moreover, will make it more likely that you achieve what you want to achieve. When you know yourself you are able to make better choices about everything, from what sandwich you will buy to bigger and more important ones, like which partner you will spend your life with.

You will gain guidelines and automatically solve problems coming your way. When your actions reflect your feelings and values, you will experience less inner conflict. You will understand the motivations you have, resist bad habits but also develop new and good ones. You will have pure insight into which values and goals activate your willpower. At some point you need to learn how to resist social pressure. When you are grounded in your values and preferences, you are less likely to say yes when you were initially about to say no.

Your awareness of your own struggles can help you empathise with others. All you need to learn is how to tolerate and understand others. Then, when you finally know who you truly are, it will help you to feel more alive and make your life experience richer and more exciting. It is hard, and always will be. It is a learning process after all, and you are constantly changing. Society's values quite often conflict with your own. For all of us, and I start with me, being yourself sounds easier than it actually is in the physical world you live in. You get distracted and lose sight of what is actually true and lies behind you, and there you are again; the past taught you otherwise.

It has put you in a position you thought you were meant to be in, but never satisfied or fully completed. The answer is clear; you have not found yourself yet. But there is hope, and it is easier than most of you think. Changing your way of thinking and dealing with every day, even when life catches up, you can guide yourself to become who you truly are. Then suddenly, you no longer conform to how you should think, act and also feel.

You have made a discovery; an act of self-knowledge will give you energy and save you in return. A true feeling of comfort. Certain things or values such as helping those in need, living a healthy life style, feeling secure in your surroundings, or living a creative life style can motivate you and it will guide you back to who you are. When you know your values, you find self-motivation. Why not find a hobby, a passion for anything that draws your attention over a period of time? At times when your busy life style takes over, all you need to do is ask yourself what you enjoy, what you are curious about. When you focus on your interests, your life becomes vivid and gives you clues to your deepest passion.

Finding what you love brings love into every aspect of your life. Many of you build a career from things which motivate you or leave you with a passion for. We are likely to choose work in a sector where we had good experiences. Imagine if you had such an amazing time when you were in school that you decide to become a teacher. How do you restore your energy should be the next question. Are you enjoying time amongst others or do you prefer time by yourself?

Do you make decisions more from feelings and thoughts or more from facts? Are you really going with the flow and letting destiny take over? Do you trust the process and let it all go or are you working for what you think you desire? When going through a tough time in the past, were you showing gratitude or falling into depression and self-hate? There are a lot of answers when you ask your good old inner self what the most meaningful event in your life has been so far. You discover clues to your hidden identity, your career, your contentment with life in general, but mostly you will find what has made you who you are to date.

When you see your talents and work on your character strengths, such as being respectful, loyal, fair, showing love, or having emotional intelligence, you know who you are. Learning to accept the bad in the same way as the good, listening to the words of others, and acknowledging skills you have could not only be clues to your strengths, but also your weaknesses. When you know your weaknesses, you are naturally more honest with yourself and others around you.

It is hugely important not to deny who you are. How many of you work in a Monday to Friday corporate job, living in conflict with your core values but still denying the reality of the situation? There is no more greater fulfilment than knowing your purpose here on this planet and starting to plant the seeds for it. You are who you are. The earlier in life you accept this and get on with it, the easier your life will be.

Let us all finally start embracing it instead of hiding under the covers. Always remember when you work in the will of the source who has planned this learning journey for you long before you touched ground and knows who you are, he and the whole universe will work magic to bring you to the place you belong. It is perfectly fine to explore what your heart wants. It is completely ok to tune out the rest of the world to build a connection with your soul.

Find the person living within yourself. Knowing yourself is the process of understanding what kind of human being you are on a deeper level. It is an unpredictable road that you must be willing to explore. It brings you face to face with your deep self-doubts and insecurities. It makes you take a serious look at the way you are living your life and put it to question.

It will take a while, but in the end it will all be worth it because of the abundance that will be showered from the universe. Knowing yourself means respecting your values in life, your beliefs, personality, priorities, moods, habits and getting to know your body as well as your personal relationships. Knowing yourself means understanding your desires and dreams. Knowing what purpose in life you have to fulfil before returning back home.

Chapter 3: It comes all from within

When it comes to your emotions, it is understandable outside circumstances greatly influence them. When good things happen, you feel good. It is so easy. When bad things happen, you feel bad. You are only human, and you naturally have a preference for pleasant situations occurring. When you really want to start making changes in your life, and feel happier, you have to do your best not to let the outside rule the inside; you have to turn it around. What is happening inside will reflect what is happening outside, and you want to work on trying to feel good now, regardless of what is happening.

You can't tell yourself you will feel better when life throws unpleasant situations. Living re-actively gives away your power but it teaches you important lessons, even if you don't see them at this exact moment. Happiness is alone in yourself, meaning if you wish to be happy, despite what is going on around you and even if you want a cheap escape, you have to keep doing things that make you happy. There is no need to feel eternally grateful, but happy about the things going on around you.

The moment things don't go your way you grow; you find freedom but also fulfilment. We do feel that is the moment when darkness overcomes and covers all the light we have been shining out from within, but we don't see that this is the part of personal growth. The world does not end; you only pick yourself up and keep walking. A feeling of hurt or loss doesn't come from the outside world, it is all in you. Even if you are not, you are ready. Everything is within you. One of the strongest and most powerful feelings is Love; it was, is and always will be inside you. It is one of those emotions you sometimes prefer not to have, but you do.

Love has been set as a main subject and given to you automatically long before your soul touched ground. It is divine and within you. This emotion can't go away or disappear. It is simply the most powerful one, and there is a lot you can do with it. When you come to a place of no return, Love is what you bring with you. When a sense of loss arises, something knocked Love down. Sometimes you need to learn it is appropriate to let grief in.

The magic is thought to remove it, or skip over it and not give it its due. The best you can do is get up and let it go. You don't have to carry grief within you.

When it comes to Love, choose Love because Love is absolutely built in. Love comes from within as mentioned before and will walk over grief, if you allow it. Anything else that disturbs your peace of mind is a hitchhiker; you can drop off a hitchhiker. You don't have to give a hitchhiker a free ride. If you already picked one up, you can easily drop him off. You have to let go of what you don't want to keep to yourself. You don't have to keep something you don't want. Whatever negativity assails you, you have to be done with it. Turn your mind in a different direction and reap joy. Every great dream begins with a dreamer.

You have to remember that within you is the patience, the strength and the passion to reach positivity and the stars to change your own world. The more you are, the more you can become and the more you can become, the more you can yet be. Passion that comes from the heart doesn't keep love apart. Memories of your troubled past do not last; you awaken from a deep sleep. The past hurt is done; now you can move on. At times your own light goes out and is rekindled by a spark from another person. Each of you has cause to think with deep gratitude of those who have relit the flame within you.

We have to learn how to get in touch with the silence within ourselves, knowing everything in life has purpose. There are no mistakes, no coincidences. Every single event is a blessing, given to you to learn from. People are like stained glass windows; they sparkle and shine when the sun is out, but when the darkness sets in, their true beauty is revealed only if there is a light from within. People can't be changed by you; you can only help them discover the light within themselves. The only journey, your own journey, is the one within. You see the truth is within, the true power is within and it is available to you at any time.   That is the reason you need to live in the present.

Everything surrounding you is what is within you. The pure and unconditional love you can feel within yourself is the happiness which springs up from within. You believe what you see and in return, you believe your interpretation of what you see.   Most of the time we don't even realise that we are making an interpretation. Everything you have is already inside yourself, though you only recognise certain bits relating to the current stage of your path. Real happiness comes from the self, and it can only be found in the self.

If you learn how to be your own best friend then you will find true happiness, because happiness is from within. If you are unaware of what is within, you will be shown a mirror of your near future life experience. You have powerful tools, tools to choose. They are free and within you now. They are the tools to conscious thoughts. To discover who you truly are, you must stop searching for truth in the outer world and instead go within and experience it personally, openly and sincerely. You have the power over your own mind, not the outside events. When you realise this, you will find strength. Nothing can dim the light which shines from within.

Anything that is happy and at peace you mistake for weakness. It is not your job to change others, but it can be your job to show that your peace and gentleness do not equate to weakness. The sun shines not on you but in you. Everything you achieve inwardly will change your outer reality.

You might get knocked down on the outside, but the key to living in victory is to learn how to get up on the inside. You are one thing only; you are a divine being, a powerful creator. You have to rely on whatever sparks you from the inside.

When you beautify your inner world with love, light and compassion, your life will be beautiful. Meditation is realising and expanding your inner beauty in every direction. You will be amazed what is achievable with your own power. So many of us walk around feeling powerless; we procrastinate and fail to apply yourself to the work before us. Failing to control your weight. Fearing rejection and failing to start a conversation when needed. You shrink from confronting others; you can't even reach your full humanity without some exercise of power. How do you experience yourself as authentically powerful? This is what you should ask yourself.

Authentic power is about self-governance. Facing adversity to overcome fear and inhibition, to be sufficiently in touch with your inner lives that you are genuinely able to express yourself and chart your life's direction, to be open to a range of interpersonal relationships, to be assertive without being confrontational, and to create the meaning of your own Life. As you are not born with it, you won't get there without struggles. But once you have it, you don't keep it forever. You have to continue to struggle to maintain it. The possession of authentic power will be an on-going process. Authentic power is not the same thing as worldly power. It is often difficult to find those who feel authentically powerful, who feel anything like inner strength or a sense of being in command of themselves. It could even be harder to identify people who experience themselves as genuinely powerful among those apparently powerful people. Most of you are neither powerless nor totally powerful but have some combination of weakness and strengths. Dominance is not the same thing as authentic power. In fact, those who rely on dominating others to establish their own self esteem are often papering over an underlying sense of weakness, and often doubt whether they are authentically loved or even liked.

A certain amount of strength is required for you to open yourself up and express vulnerability. Authentic power wells up from within. Power is seen as a win or lose kind of relationship. Power within has to do with a person's sense of self-worth and self-knowledge. It is an ability to recognise individual differences while respecting others. Power within is the capacity to imagine and have hope. You all have special powers; the only reason why you are not living the life you want is because you don't know how to use those special powers.

It is the power from within and once you learn how to apply this power that you have within yourself, you will be able to dramatically change or improve your life faster than you thought possible. How can you start using your power from within? First you have to learn how to direct your subconscious mind to attract the people and situations that will help you create the changes or improvements in life you want. Then you have to begin changing how you see things, but also how you see yourself. If you want love, you have to love yourself. If you want a healthy and caring relationship, you have to be someone who is healthy and caring with yourself. If you want to be successful, you have to see yourself as someone who is capable of being successful.

You can no longer accept any limitations of negative thoughts and beliefs that prevent you from accomplishing your goals. Only you can determine your own success. It doesn't matter if people around you are negative. You don't need encouragement and support from others. All you need it to believe and see yourself as someone who is capable of all you wish to become. Now you can begin to direct your subconscious mind so that it begins attracting beautiful opportunities for you to be successful.

All you need to do is take a look at where you are today and decide what kind of life you want. Once you see yourself as successful, you will be able to direct your conscious mind and subconscious mind to start using your power within to help you achieve goals. The next step is to develop a higher level of self-awareness. Most people are not aware of the power within that they possess. Most don't know why things happen the way they do; they simply accept that they happened and that is the end of it. They are missing out on an opportunity to work with their power from within.

When you are more aware you not only realise what you want and where you are heading, but also how to get there. It is like giving your power within a set of instructions to follow. It is very important that to get results, you must not complain. We attract what we give out. If you put focus on what is wrong and complain, you attract the same back -people who complain. This creates negativity. You have to stop thinking what is wrong in your life and focus on all you have; be thankful for the little things and work on them to build them up.

With the change of your mind-set, you will attract people and situations to help and guide you in the right direction; those who won't serve you anymore will have less of an impact on your life and ambitions. Your mind-set is a powerful tool and it has always been inside, within you. Everything comes from within, and as soon you realise what you are made of and what you can achieve, you will be able to find who you are and what huge things you can achieve if you believe in your own power.

Chapter 4: The mind as a powerful tool

The power of the mind is one of the greatest secrets of the world. Scientists all over the world have been seeking knowledge for decades, but no one really understands that this great power can only be found within. The subconscious mind is responsible for all of our deepest emotions, motivations and expectations. We do not fully realise the power of our own mind. Once you understand that you can train your subconscious, you have a whole new way to look at life. You begin to realise there is untapped potential lying right inside your mind.

The biggest factor for you to understand, when it comes to subconscious programming, is the realisation that thoughts are powerful. All you have to do is believe in what you think and allow those thoughts to come to fruition. Since this is the first step in any creative process, it would be fitting that you gear your thoughts in the right direction. Only when your thoughts are powerful will the result of those thoughts determine the final outcome. All your thoughts will, in the end, produce those same results, whether good or bad. In order to comprehend this better, all you need to do is examine your thoughts more extensively. They are always in alignment with the universe; we are all created by the Source and came into this timeline still being connected subconsciously, with the creator. Made for guidance and protection, it is you who needs to learn how to listen. Thoughts are very powerful. If you examine people around you and take a good look at how they appear and what they do, you will, more or less, get an idea about what they were thinking. Ever heard the saying, "Be careful what you wish for"? In your case, be careful what you think about. If you think prosperity, you will receive prosperity.

If you think poverty, you will reap poverty. What you think about, you will manifest. It is not merely a decision to alter what you allow into your conscious; you also have to change what is already in your subconscious. This is because your previous thoughts entered into and were processed by your subconscious mind. Some who do not believe will not allow themselves to change, because they only accept what they can see. Others have taken on the responsibility of change, found the truth about their thoughts and how these thoughts made them as a person as well as what they experience at this precise moment in time. Therefore, they began to understand the power of the mind and of thoughts and now use this to their advantage to produce what they desire. What you think you produce, what you conceive you manifest. If there is something you do not like, you should not think about it. If you have a true belief that what you want to happen will happen, and you have the emotion behind it, you will be the vibration of your thoughts, match the frequency of the universe, and the universe will respond, since you attract what you think about.

Sometimes it takes a tragic event to change your perception, and it forces you to make changes. It can affect, good and bad, as thoughts have the power to be creative. Think for yourself. No one can think for you. No one can attract things into your life, only you can. Thoughts are very powerful; you can accomplish so much with your thoughts. You can invent and create. You can do or be whatever you want. It only takes one thought. As long as you are in unity with the universal law, you should not have any trouble achieving what you want. The mind is unlimited in potential. You can create anything you desire just by letting the mind do what it was created for. You do not need to struggle in life to make something of yourself. As I have already spoken about, life does have a purpose for you. It will give you Abundance if you program your mind in the right direction. Once you learn and apply the principles and techniques required to alter your programming, enhance your mind functions and improve the way your mind can develop, you can have all that you wish for or desire. All it takes is a single step and an understanding of the mechanism to appreciate what it does. In the average person it is proven that we only use 10% of the brain, leaving 90% not utilised.

Every person has the same capacity, but not everyone is using it. It is the choices you make and the beliefs you were programmed with that separate successful from unsuccessful individuals. Believing and having faith are what allow you to take part, or not, in events in your life. You got where you are because you knew the power of the human mind and you utilised it to its fullest. Again, you have to be aware of what you want. The next step is to desire what you want. The tricky part is the pre-processed programming or beliefs. If your beliefs allow the situation to occur, it will.

The idea of subconscious programming is important; it is the mechanism by which your old thought processes can be changed so you will have new beliefs. As a matter of fact, there have been great studies carried out which showed people accomplishing important feats with the power of their mind. Acknowledging this power and using it beneficially is what will help you take the first step toward realising your goal and obtaining whatever it is you want. The universe wants to give you everything you wish for and to reach all in life. Open your mind to the world, and see the immense power it has. In order to do this, you first need to tap into your subconscious.

Developing the understanding of the power of the mind starts with knowing two laws of principles- the law of vibration and the law of attraction. The law of vibration seems easy to understand, but can be complicated to those who do not understand how it works. The one principle we will take away is that this law will always be here among us and always work, whether we choose to believe it or not. It states that everything in the universe, no matter what it may be, is energy. Energy makes up the universe. Everything vibrates at different rates or speeds.

When the vibration is within our ability or frequency range, you can hear or see the vibrating source of energy. Because you were created by some infinite spirit, this higher power vibrates too. And since you are part of this creation or consciousness, you are also energy in the form of a body. You vibrate like anything else. Every part of you is a vibration including your thoughts. You become aligned with the universe in vibration. You are able to attract whatever the vibrations point to. Your thoughts, which go back to your conscious and subconscious, must vibrate in tune with the universe in order for you to achieve what you wish for. This is why it is important to monitor your inner thoughts to make sure you are in harmony with the universe.

The law of attraction is an universal law that states that there is a cause and effect to everything you think and do. If you think about a particular thing, you end up getting it. Just as it is important to learn about the law of vibration, you must also learn about the law of attraction. You have to make sure your subconscious thoughts are geared toward what you are trying to attract. If they are not, you will not achieve it. It is universal and never goes away.

You can control it to some degree by what you vibrate to. The end result is simple; if you reprogram your subconscious mind to vibrate with the universe, you can get anything you want just by thinking of it. You always attract the same vibration to you as the vibration you are. You attract the same likeminded people into your life. Everything you want, you can attract to you. The magic is to clear your mind and to truly think about what you really want, not only need in a specific situation in life. Let it go and trust the universe.

Chapter 5:

Wanting and needing are different emotions

Needing and wanting something are different emotions many of you do not understand or agree with. What you want might not be necessarily what you need. Humanity takes mostly the example of friendships or romantic relationships. There is a major difference between wanting someone because you think you desire them and needing them because you desire them from a place of insecurity or possession.

This can also be seen as controlling someone because you fear hurt, or feel unwanted because of their own free will, choice, and desire. True and real love is based upon your time and your heart for the sole purpose of contributing to the happiness, welfare and wellbeing of another unconditionally, without any attachments of getting something in return. There should be a sense of freedom, but also oneness, between souls involved. There is a purpose for all relationships.

Giving and not taking in order to fill yourself up with what you feel you lack. All of you accept the love you think you deserve. Love is when you want what you need and need what you want.

Love is a choice, but you should never settle for less. Unfortunately, you don't get to choose if you get hurt. How your mind and heart deals with a situation will be the outcome. Remember the mind is a powerful tool, and you can not only climb mountains but also control feelings and learn from situations. There is a way of loving someone, and of course needing them should be a factor. All relationships have varying degrees of needs supporting them; however the higher the percentage of these needs in the relationship, the less likely it is to be healthy. Out of need, many of you go into bad relationships that don't really suit you, and then you end up with a breakup.

The moment needing shows up love will end, because the relationship is only based on that emotion. If you go into a relationship just because you were feeling lonely, as soon as your social life becomes better you will find yourself not in need of it anymore and the relationship will fall apart. The difference between wanting someone and needing someone can clearly ruin your thinking of attracting love and the affection with it. When you fall in love to escape from your day to day problems, to reduce bad moods, to feel better about yourself and so on, then you will need the relationship instead of wanting it.

The moment you find someone who clicks all your heart's desires boxes and matches the criteria you wish to find in a future partner, you will truly fall in love. If you are feeling down, lonely or broken from inside and in a desperate need to feel appreciated or loved, then you might go for the wrong person just to satisfy this need even if you don't really want this person. Quite often you will believe that you love someone and that you want this person so badly, while in fact you just need this individual because there is something wrong with yourself. It happens quite often - you want something, and want it for a certain amount of time. Look back at how badly you wanted something in the past. Do you really still want it now? Wants, like needs, change with time. The question is, what would remain for a longer period of time, possibly forever?

Love is the answer. It is a passion for someone. This will stay for eternity. Someone you dearly love with all your heart. Loving them no matter what. Time only makes fondness for the person grow and become stronger. What are you passionate about? What do you enjoy with all your heart? What gives you a feeling of completeness? No matter how difficult it seems, that is what makes you happy. Needing is when you like a few traits in a person. You like them for a while, and eventually the interest is gone when you find something better for yourself. Wanting is when you like them because of the way your heart feels at a precise moment and you just know it will last. As mentioned above, you accept the love you think you deserve. Over a period of time you come to realise you deserve better when the initial feeling of needing is met. You just needed it to push you to believe you deserve more. When the need is met, you move on to find something to fulfil the new need. Looking back on break ups you experienced, you will agree. Relationships that start off on a basis of needing will fall apart.

Relationships based on mutual love for each other are the ones that last. Possibly for an eternity. When you need love and meet someone who loves you, it is most likely in the end our needs will be met at some point and you will close this door. When you want love and meet someone who is in need of love, this might end in a break up as well. When you love someone and get love in return, it becomes a lasting relationship. Beautiful and pure. Needs and wants have reasons behind their approach; you might not understand that in a specific moment, but eventually when the lesson is learned it will become clear.

Every encounter in this life is planned; every person you cross paths with is heavenly sent. Some show up to teach you great lessons, some to guide you, some to fulfil you. The moment you try too hard to be happy in relationships should be a sign of being in the wrong ones. Love can and will never be replaced. At times you might find yourself looking at other couples wondering how perfectly suited relationships for decades just fall apart, as one doesn't feel love anymore. When you understand the difference between needing, loving and wanting someone you surely save yourself from unwanted pain. When there is a feeling of not loving yourself, or a feeling of needing someone to make you feel worthy, then again there is a feeling of needing.

When do you really want something? You like a certain quality in a person, you desire it, and you want to be around this individual because you like all their traits. Needing is essential in that moment and wanting is complementary. A lot of people confuse needing someone with loving them. But they are not synonymous. When you need someone, you will lose your independence as a human being. You are constantly reliant on another person. You lose the ability and desire to complete basic tasks by yourself.

You forget what it is like to be alone with your thoughts, and you can barely remember a time when you were capable of existing alone. It might sound like love but it is not. Who would want a partner which you need in your life to survive? You also don't want a partner who needs you. There has to be a healthy two way street. Falling into this neediness is not a conscious decision. It often happens quickly and discretely. Early detection of this neediness is crucial and can feel like treating yourself first class into a destination called codependency.

Wanting, on the other hand, is the step in learning how to love someone. You want to be around the other person because they make you smile, and feel happier; time just flies. There is no need for them to be there when you sit, read or watch a program on television. You can do this all by yourself. While you are fully capable of completing tasks alone, you like having the other person there with you. You don't need them to be, you just want them to be. When you want someone in your life, you want them there because life is more exciting and fun with them on your side. You want them because you are a complete person without them; you are able to stand alone.

Loving someone is much more beautiful and rewarding then leaning on them for everything.

Chapter 6:

What you get is what you gave – Karma

What you get is what you gave, receiving what you deserve. Present actions or some from your past will always reflect on you, in this world or in a metaphysical one. It is based on logic, a consequence of your creation. If you get angry and do another harm, then you create a state in which you are harming another. You create a state in which you are happy with the suffering of another. You also create a state in which another is unhappy and is suffering. You create a state in which you are joyful that your enemy is harmed.

Another state in when someone is resentful and angry about those who have been wrongly treated. Any thoughts you have, whether with good intention or bad, produce Karmic effects. How beautiful would a world be where no one is harming another? In the end it is all a result of your own creation. The result of this past action is called Karma and it is present now. You create your own

Karma, in this very moment. Out of habit you create good, but also bad, Karma. It doesn't exist in the past as a thing to reward or punish you. You can create Karma though, good Karma with positive thoughts and actions. All you think, act and speak unconsciously creates Karma. In order to have the good and not the bad, you need to change your habits and see the good in every situation occurring. It has to start within you; accept yourself. When you intend to understand each other, you create understanding and the result is tolerance. When you wish others well, you create a state of being wished well. This for sure is acceptable to all. By creating a state of being happy, happiness will take place. The final habit to change is the creation of respecting another. What you create is being respected, which makes the circle complete. "Do to others what you would like them to do to you".

Karma is a divine law; it is natural. It shouldn't be seen as punishment. It is fair and applies to everyone who creates. It can't be avoided. It is the essence of divine simplicity itself, while manifesting can be highly complex. In the everyday, humans put out "what goes around comes around", which is a loose but nevertheless truthful description of Karma. Each lesson is perfectly tailored to your spiritual needs. There will never be a test given to you that you wouldn't be able to pass. It only gives you experience, the perfect opportunity to learn living in harmony with your soul.

When you learn, you advance. It is a chance to come closer to higher spiritual states of consciousness, but mostly to enjoy great freedom. You have to remember there is "good Karma" but also "bad Karma". To most of us this becomes meaningless, as our mind-set is built to only see the bad when things fall apart, yet actually happen for the good. We all have the power to change our Karma for better or for worse. It is simply dependent on our thoughts and actions. Whatever thoughts and actions you think or observe you receive or get back, sooner or later. Because of this, every second in your lives you are determining what your future Karma will be. If you have done wrong, as we all have as some point, then by doing the right now, you can burn up the negative "bad" Karma and create a positive "good" one.

It is not that easy to work out someone's Karma by looking at their life. In general, spiritually advanced people consciously, or also unconsciously, choose to go through terrible suffering in order to burn up their negative Karma as quickly as possible. The more good you do, the more good will be available to you; hence the thing to remember about Karma is the importance of service to others. The more good you do the more opportunities you will be given to do good, whether it will be in this life or a future life time. If your positive Karma manifested as wealth, which is entirely possible depending on your Karmic patterns, then you should not look at it as, "What a good person I must have been in the past; therefore now I am going to enjoy using what has come to me to satisfy my own desires without worrying about anyone else around me". The right way to look at it would be, "It is great I got what came towards me. I can use it to help others". Karma simply means action- no more, no less. It is a law of action and reaction. Karma is the pattern that keeps maintaining itself, so one can also say that Karma is what keeps the world going round, more or less.

It is simply the way in which the seeds you sow in your life tend to create similar results. If you sow seeds of health, harmony and goodness you are likely to reap crops of the same type. By sowing seeds of harm, exploitation and self-centredness, you are likely to face similar things in your life. Action and reaction happens, but the system is so huge that it also gives you a lot of freedom. Karma offers a position that is neither total chaos nor a deterministic world, working clockwise, but somewhere in between. You have the power to break the circle, the habit and change the conditions- to clean up your act. You can sow the best seeds and hopefully reap the best fruit in this life, if you pay attention to what you are doing. You can watch Karma happening as the things you do in your world roll on and on. It is creating results in the most unexpected places. One lie which we tell can make a big mess and do harm to ourselves or others. It will make you feel guilty, uncomfortable and agitated; it can and will steal your peace and joy. If you watch this process carefully you can see the wheels of Karma rolling, and know that you must be caring, wise and responsible in all your thoughts and words, but also in your deeds.

Chapter 7: Knowing and trusting the process

Trusting the process means knowing and having faith that there is a divine plan moving through you and your life in any given moment. Even if you cannot understand the unfolding behind the scenes right now, you should have an unshakeable sense of trust. Trusting and knowing it is happening for your higher good. Before this happens, there might be some dramatic shift unfolding in your life, usually arising as a result of you making an inner spiritual shift or important life changing decision. It is happening, without you being aware. When you say yes to your inner guidance and allow it to unfold, magic happens.

Your ego at times can be quite loud and tell you the reverse, but when you learn how to deal with that feeling you allow your true inner self to come out, and a feeling of knowing covers your soul. Your life will change for the better in that given moment. Scary at times but when you realise why this has to happen, a profound sense of calmness will cover not only your soul but also your ego. It is important to place a deep faith in your angelic guidance team behind the scenes, which is the same as a sense of trust in the unknown.

Knowing and trusting the process is a beautiful phrase, but you also have to live it. When you stand vulnerable with all that you think, you are forced to practice, live in the present and breathe that profound level of trust. An opportunity to implement, practise and embody everything you have to come to know will show up. When you trust the process, you allow the realm of the intangible to guide your ship and lead you step by step on your journey. When you have a good and stable relationship with yourself, faith is much easier to practise. All of us, at some certain moments in time, have struggled with faith and with a feeling of the unknown. Trust that if you let go of your inner demons, you will be safe and your needs will be met.

It is important to remember that when you know who you are, as mentioned earlier on, you will have faith in yourself and that means putting your faith into the unknown. Trusting requires closing away your outer awareness and bringing peace inwards. There will be a knowing in that moment of beauty and completeness; the inside is more real than anything you can touch, see or even experience on the outside. Faith alone is built on that knowing. It is also called truth. The knowing of your own truth.

When you live moment by moment throughout your life, you build trust unconsciously. When you walk with faith, you walk with feeling. The decisions you make there are based on inner whispers, the energy that tugs at your heart and calls you towards what you love.

In my first book, "Her whispers - she never left my side", I wrote about this little voice, the whisper. Guardian Angels or Spirit Guides put a certain feeling or voice inside your ear for you to understand what the best desired outcome will be. I personally had many encounters with my Angels guiding me towards happiness and completeness. Many lessons had to be learned, and I am still on a learning path. Life is full of lessons, day in and out, but you can trust and know you are never alone, as the guidance provided to you is heavenly sent. We are all spiritual beings in a human body living to serve, to give but also to receive love. You came here for a reason and the guidance you get is the pathway you are supposed to be on to fulfil your purpose in this life time. You don't have to be an Angelic believer to understand that you are watched over and protected. All you need is to listen to your true self, your dreams and your visions. It is irrelevant what others say or see; to live with faith is to know who you are.

The best practise you can do is to close your eyes and feel the desires. When energy of who you are moves through your body, it will guide you on your path. There is no need of knowing, seeing or controlling everything right now. You don't need to know what is going to happen. Letting it all go and trusting is all you need. Every day you make major and minor choices that affect your future. The choices you make influence not only your spiritual and emotional but also physical health, and affect the ones closest to you. Your choices have deep power.

A simple decision to stop an addiction can have a positive ripple effect, greater than you could imagine. A thoughtless decision can carry just as much harm. The reason why you make those decisions comes out of fear. It is the moment you speak up, when you follow your dreams you allow this fear to stop. Fear is an unconscious feeling stopping you from finding peace from within. It is important to remember that no matter how many poor choices you have made in the past, you always have the freedom to choose again. Life doesn't come with a guarantee. It is simply a process you can choose to trust. Choosing change from within and going with the flow brings power and self-acceptance. Life will always support you if you allow it.

You should never deny feelings. Painful emotions will pass through you. You need to learn to detach from people, places and things no longer serving you. When you believe in your own abilities, you will respond to the life given to you. You survived so many things in the past. It is important you move in a new direction. Decide for yourself that you will survive. Life can easily catch up and put everything against you; the magic is to find a way forward. When you live with a positive attitude, your heart will be grateful. Power comes from being responsible; facing your fears will overcome them. When you remember you are exactly where you are supposed to be, you remove distractions and find the path where you want to go. Realising this is a gift in trusting the unseen.

When you are willing to change your plans and direction, you are open to the not knowing. You have to let go of your fear of change and believe the best is yet to come. Always remember, the dark doesn't last forever. When you allow enjoyment of your day to day, you claim abundance and see the light become visible right in front of you. When you trust the process of life, you connect with a sense of unconditional love and oneness. The path called life becomes clear and you will feel at home and safe.

Every bad experience or painful relationship will transform you into a beautiful inner reservoir of spiritual gifts and blessings. Life wants you to take notice of trusting, changing and believing. Sometimes when you lose your way, you find yourself. Lessons learned last a lifetime. If love doesn't last it, prepares you for the one that will. Sometimes it takes a wrong turn to get you to the right place. Life is not meant to be lived perfectly, but it is to be lived. What you are waiting for is not as important as what happens to you while you are waiting. Not everyone will see your dreams and visions. You have to know and believe for yourself.

The stretching of your faith is immediate pain that results in ultimate gain. It is in the waiting that you become who you are meant to be. In the midst of your struggle to find out who you are, and there are infinite possibilities for beauty, hope, wonder and love. You have to trust what feels true even if that truth requires you to ignore what you know. Things always make sense in hindsight. When you look back on your life, you can see that you went through the exact challenges that were necessary to allow growth in the precise way that you most needed it.

All your personal struggles led you exactly where you really wanted to go, but didn't know at that time. How difficult was it for you to let go? Everything in your life really is happening for your greater good. The problem is that you forget this in the midst of pain. You forget this in the midst of wanting what you think you want in this specific moment. You forget this when you can't see evidence of it. The evidence is there. Look at your past, and write a list of all the ways you are grateful that your life didn't work out the way you had planned or hoped. Write a list afterwards of everything you are grateful for that you never even knew you wanted but have today. Putting both lists together will give you faith. You have to look at the bigger picture and remember you are enough, good enough.

Trust the process; it is all good, even though it feels bad. You are going exactly where you are meant to go. Despite evidence to the contrary, the universe is conspiring in your favour. Visualise the outcome; when you imagine how it would feel to be in the situation as it unfolds, and witness the outcome you believe, it will occur. After you visualise the outcome, it is important to take a step back and think about this particular situation in the grand scale of your lifetime.

How will it affect your future? It is all about putting things into perspective and understanding; if the first plan doesn't work out, the next one might be the one you got prepared for. When it comes to trusting the process and letting go, all you have to do is move on to the next new thing. Life always has an amazing way of working out, believe it or not.

Chapter 8: Forgiving and healing

Forgiveness is the power to choose how daily events affect you, the admitting of all offences occurred in your life. Forgiveness is only appropriate when an offence has been committed and the offence has caused damage. The moment an offence has been committed against you, it is critical to recognise and admit the reality of this offence. Overcoming denial might be difficult, but it is essential. Forgiveness does not ignore the reality of an offence, but validates that the offence did occur in your life. You benefit immensely when you choose to forgive. It is not only for you, but also everyone around you.

Whether you need to forgive others or yourself, doing so sets you free from the past and enables you to fulfil your true potential. Forgiveness allows you to break free from limiting beliefs and attitudes. It certainly frees up your mental and emotional energies so that you can apply them to create a better life, full of joy and pure happiness. Forgiveness helps you to achieve even your most practical and immediate goals. Better relationships, a better income or a better job. Forgiveness helps you to achieve all of it.

If you have not forgiven, then a part of your inner life energy is trapped in resentment, pain and a feeling of not only suffering but also anger. This energy will limit you; it will slow down the process of manifesting what you truly desire. Frustration will take place and that will make it difficult to move forward. Choices you make and things you believe are possible, but they will all be influenced by the ways you have not forgiven. As you learn to forgive, the energy which was going into unhappy thoughts and feelings gets liberated and can flow into creating the life you want rather than limiting you.

If you do not want to learn to forgive for your own benefit, then learning to forgive can benefit others. As you learn to forgive, you benefit everyone you are in contact with. Your thinking will be clearer and more positive than it was before. You will have a lot more to give and you will more readily enjoy sharing what you have already. You become kinder, more generous and more caring of others. The attitude on the outside will be more positive. Always remember what you give out you get back in return. A forgiving person is easier to be around then an unforgiving one. The quality of your life depends on the quality of your relationships.

Every aspect of your life will change for the better as you learn to forgive, whether in your work life or social one. Learning to forgive will improve all your relationships, because your attitude will be different. As a conclusion, when your relationships improve all aspects of your life will improve. If you want to move up to the next level of success, forgiveness will help to achieve it. If you wish more financial security in your life, you need to make sure that you don't resent people who have more financial security than you. You have to be open to receiving, rather than resenting them.

If you have a positive attitude towards people who are more successful than you, they will see you as approachable and will more likely want to work or socialise with you. If you want a better job or earn more money, then having a positive attitude towards the place you work, towards your manager, towards colleagues and clients or customers helps immensely. People who have a positive, helpful attitude stand out. You can never succeed in an organisation which you do not want to succeed, because you will not give your best. If you do not give your best or do the best job you can, then you will not receive the best that can come to you.

Forgiveness will help you have the attitude which makes you very successful where you are at present, or where you want to be. Learning to forgive yourself plays a huge importance in it. Hurting yourself, by refusing to forgive yourself, hurts others around you also. If you do not forgive yourself, you will punish yourself by denying yourself the good things in life. The more you deny yourself, the less you have to give. The less you have to give, the less you can benefit those around you. When you stop limiting what you receive, then you stop limiting what you can give. Everyone benefits when you forgive yourself as you then allow better into your life, and have a lot more to share. When you forgive you are more open to success in whatever ways are meaningful to you.

As you learn to forgive what seemed impossible not only becomes possible, but can even become easily achievable. Spiritually minded people, like me, learn practical ways to forgive. It will enhance and deepen your experience of spiritual practise. It will help free you from guilt about not being as good as you feel you should be; it will help you become the person you would like to be. Practising forgiveness strengthens the goodness within you. As an outcome it becomes more active in your life.

Naturally, you will feel less inclined to do things you know you should not do but have not been able to stop yourself doing. As you start to do more of the things you know you are good at, you find your way back to the beginning and remember clearly your life purpose. Learning to forgive can only help you; it certainly cannot hurt you. Forgiveness is immensely practical and helpful. There is nothing vague or impractical about it. Forgiveness sets you free. As you learn to forgive, many problems will gradually disappear. It will be as if you can view your life from above and see the easiest way to get where you want to be. Life will open up in front of you in the most magical ways. New opportunities will emerge as if from nowhere.

Happy coincidences will occur where you meet just the right person at just the right time. Ideas or answers will come to you just as you need them. A friend may make a comment, or you flip open a book or a magazine, or you may overhear a conversation which gives you just what you were looking for. Why is this so? It is because by practicing forgiveness you become more open to the goodness of life, so that goodness is more able to find its way to you.

The book I wrote and published in the last year, "Her Whispers - she never left my side", gives many examples of those miracles. The book is about the unconditional love between my grandmother and me, and the relationship we had from the day I was born until heaven opened the doors to welcome and introduce her to a peaceful place. She gave signs of her presence, showing me the loving Guardian Angel she became with the guidance she gave on a daily basis. Spirit guides are real, and they stay with us throughout our existence to offer protection, to hold, to comfort and make us understand we are in this timeline for a reason - to serve, to give, but also to receive love in the highest interest of the source.

I started helping others who were in a similar situation as I was before; people who lost a special someone but always felt their presence. People feel lost in transition and confused, but it could be so simple to read the Angelic messages. It is time we all hear them clearly, but there is loads to work on beforehand, as talked about in the previous chapters. Forgiving is healing; healing opens doors to be a better version of ourselves. As we learn to forgive, abilities which have been dormant within us will emerge, and we will discover we are much stronger and more capable than we previously imagined. Parts of you which could not thrive in the frigid soil of unforgiveness will start to grow. You will begin to let go of struggling and striving. You will find more of an easy flow and life will be a lot more pleasant and enjoyable. Some of you carry a lot of resentments, hatred and bitterness, and suffer from psychosomatic illnesses and disorders. Those illnesses come from both mind and emotional stresses, and take their toll and manifest in the physical body. Such illnesses are manifested through mental and emotional breakdown, resulting diseases and elevated blood pressure resulting to strokes and a lot more.

Some relationships require healing and one of the most effective strategies is to find healing through forgiveness. Forgiveness has unique ways and wonderful secrets to follow in the healing process. All you need to do is release it in your heart and apologize to the other one who has hurt you, even if you don't get anything back. Your part will be done, and the soul's pain will close.

You need to rest and restore, to return mentally to that specific moment in time to face the situation that caused you this pain, but imagine a different outcome. You clear away guilt, and build a base of freedom around yourself. Restitution is unconditional. Even when the offender refuses to ask forgiveness from you, you should forgive them inside your heart. It is a process of learning; it keeps on and on. Finding healing through forgiveness can be a long way to go, but the most rewarding one. Memories will flash back; pain will flood in and sometimes bring back the same reactions one had at the moment when the pain was inflicted. It might seem forgiveness is not taking place, and we even lose faith. But exactly in this moment, forgiveness takes place. You choose to release pain each time you remember to ask for forgiveness.

Chapter 9: Cutting cords

There is a certain amount of freedom you experience - indescribable, beautiful, uplifting - and extra peace of mind when you let go of unwanted baggage and become free emotionally. In a world where you tend to believe only in that which you can physically see, such psychic cords of attachment go unnoticed and so you tend to carry unwanted energy and connections around with you for way too long (even if the soul has closed the door). Only you can remove these for yourself.

The reason people cut cords with others is to generally move on from a situation or person and let them go energetically - this means on an energy level. People who are close, people who are in an energetic bond, have cords of energy that link one to the other. They are etheric cords. The bonding itself can be light, with just a slim cord, or you can be corded heavily to another through your chakras and have multiple thick cords that literally show your attachment - mentally, emotionally and sexually.

When you care about someone, the cording is not a problem. The cords act as a conduit to send and receive psychic energy between chakras. The more energy you send, the bigger the cords-and this is normal in any relationship. Communication between chakras is how a lot of communication happens between people. When you want to let someone go because you are not moving on, the cords and the continuing psychic energy communication can hold you back. No cord is forever and you can remove them.

Whether cords re-join is entirely up to you but when you are ready to let something or someone go, you are unlikely to want to go to the effort of re-joining the psychic ties any longer. In simple terms, you can expect to find that your mind no longer dwells upon the person because the psychic attachment has been dissolved. You will find your mind quieter and calmer; it is like clearing out a wardrobe. All those old emotions associated with that situation or person dissolve as the communication between you ends. You now have extra space in your mind to fill with something better - and you will certainly have clearer intentions.

Know that when one door closes, another better one always opens up. Cutting cords can be done with anything really - people who are bothersome to you psychically, anyone who sends you strong energy and intrudes upon your thoughts and emotions even when you are alone. If you are done with someone or something, but find they always seem to intrude on your thoughts and you can feel them around you or they are simply in your mind, you can cut the connection by cutting those etheric cords that attach the both of you.

Some people with strong heart bonds can also find relief here by disconnecting their heart chakra from the other's. If an old flame was harmful or hurtful to you in some way, being free on all levels is incomparable. You literally move on and a new space is formed around you. You can then proceed to fill that space with more pleasant feelings and thoughts. If anyone has abused you emotionally or physically, you can cut the cords. Cutting these bonds will aid much faster healing. This will help to release the pain and clear out your energy field or the aura of that trauma. If a cord cutting fails, this indicates that you are not willing to really let someone or something go. Not just yet.

This is fine; it just means you are not truly ready to move on. There might be a lesson for you still to master, and your actual attachment is giving you the opportunity to learn the lesson now, and for good. One of the most important things you can do for two or more parties is to cut cords that still bind you to previous relationships and prevent you from completing those relationships in the highest of ways.

Most people do not realise that when you have a relationship with someone, your energy systems become connected, especially when there is a strong emotional or mental event between the parties such as a traumatic or painful event. You create energy cords when you make conscious or subconscious vows, contracts or promises, sometimes even unspoken, with the other party or parties. It happens often that one person will strongly feel and think that those promises remain valid to this day. The frequency of the thoughts and emotions that you had with that particular person will resonate with the energy of a specific chakra, as mentioned above. If you experienced heartbreak, then you create a cord between your heart chakra and the others person's heart chakra.

This means that even though the relationship ends, the energetic relationship is still there despite the time passed. Even though you may be physically separate now, you are still very much connected to them energetically. The same energy dynamic will go on and on if you do not cut the cord. This can drain your energy and pulse your emotional-body, depending on where the cords are located. This is why many people continue to constantly think about their previous partner and feel the pain of past events. The process of cutting cords on all levels of your awareness is the most important step to complete past relationships in the highest of ways and to remove any energetic cords that are attached between you and the other party or parties. This is the only way your soul can close the chapter and be ready to move on to higher relationships and experiences.

Not cutting cords often results in getting stuck in a low frequency relationship karmic loop where the same things keep happening over and over again. Going back to the previous example of heartbreak or betrayal, if you had these experiences during a previous relationship and you told yourself you had enough, and even though you are physically separated from this person or parties, the energetic cords from that experience will keep you connected to that person. The problem is that all the painful and traumatic experiences that you created in that relationship will then be carried in your soul memory and on to your next relationship. Those unresolved energies, or energy cords and karmic ties, will attract you to people and things that resonate with the frequency of that anger, heartbreak, or betrayal. When you do manifest another relationship, you will have a tendency to project on to your new relationship all of the hurt from the past one.

These cycles continue, and you are not aware of why all relationships fail or why you cannot attract a different type of person. You repeatedly create similar experiences. This is one of the main reasons why divorce rates dramatically increase, and ultimately this will affect your health and wellbeing. Many of those karmic relationships, often love-hate relationships, are from past lifetimes which your soul brings back into your life so that you can finally resolve and absolve the karma and move on. It is very common for some of your worst enemies from past lives to actually incarnate into your own family or come back as a future spouse.

So think about all your past relationships that have not been completed in the highest of ways and imagine if you could call up all of the karmic ties that were created from these past relationships and permanently remove all energetic attachments. Then you are able to connect with them from a place of higher giving love, gratitude and compassion in order to complete the relationship in the highest of ways. In this way, the person will not be brought back into your life later to resolve this, and/or you will not have to resolve this again in another relationship or future lifetime.

This process is exactly what has to be facilitated in order for people to cut cords. By working with your higher self, using advanced energy healing techniques, you are able to cut all karmic ties and energy cords that bind you to that previous relationship. When you clear the karmic ties and cut cords of attachments between you and your family members, it doesn't mean that you can no longer have a relationship with them. It just means that your relationship will evolve from a karmic or co-dependent one into a relationship or union of higher love and understanding. A true union is when you can love the other person and not expect anything back from them in return, and allow them to be who they are.

In this way, you have two people who are truly whole, and not just trying to extract from the other person what they feel they lack in themselves. You are also not trying to constantly change the other person. A healthy method for removing the energy cords is to imagine yourself sitting in a beautiful setting. Imagine a circle around you. The circle can be the cord. Sit in it, and feel yourself protected by it. Imagine a column of light coming from the heavens encircling you in high frequency of pure light. Then imagine the people you want out of your life also sitting in a circle made of cord.

The two circles are close to each other but not touching. Look at the other parties from your circle and wave good bye. You are gently and peacefully allowing other parties their space while affirming your own. Instead of cutting, you are transmuting the cords. Let their cords remain whole. Let your cord remain whole. Just disentangle and detach. Stoke the fires of love and compassion. Say goodbye with love and move on. As life is lived, the process of sorting and disentangling is obviously much more complex and subtle.

As you make the music of your life less dysfunctional, the people attracted to the dysfunctional part will fall off. Chords are better than cords. You are always in the process of becoming, giving birth to who you are in this moment. In this process of birthing and becoming is also the little deaths, the letting go of that which no longer serves you. This includes old relationships, old ways of acting, reacting and interacting. What if you had some way of releasing the energy that you are still putting to that which is outdated?

This one way is called cutting cords. Forgive yourself for what you think you did and let others forgive you. At some point you really have to let go. You can learn and become your own healer. You need time to process, and assimilate the work you have done. Cutting cords is a cleansing and clearing ceremony. Respect the work you have done, honour yourself and the work; allow time for yourself to have new perspectives.

Chapter 10: You are enough

You just know that feeling too well - when you've had enough of giving yourself a hard time, always comparing yourself to others, seeing that nothing you do is good enough for others around you. Enough is enough and it is time for you to let go of the negative thoughts that keep telling you that you will only be more when you work harder. It will simply keep you stuck, constantly comparing yourself to those around you. You have to understand what your body is trying to tell you when you are burning out, pushing yourself to your limits and chasing self-worth and perfectionism. You are enough.

Realizing and knowing this starts with accepting yourself. Therefore the shift to true self-acceptance is realizing you really already are enough. It does not mean that you have been measured and considered and judged when you say you are enough. You have finally earned the label of having enough. It is simply who you are, the you that is enough. You don't have to be more, or do more or buy more to be who you are meant to be. "You are enough" does not mean that you are all powerful and perfect or done with growing and changing or learning, either. It really doesn't mean that you are everything. It doesn't mean that you don't need anyone or anything else. It simply means you understand how much you do need, how small you are in this huge universe. You don't have to be even one inch bigger than that. Because you are enough. You know what your imperfection and difficulties are, but they don't reflect on your worth because you are already as you are. If being enough means being perfect, then "you are enough" is just another reason to hide your true self. You were made to be you, as you are, on purpose. It is no mistake that you are this person, in this place at this time. "You are enough" means you can grow and change and continue to become, because you are not trying to prove.

You are just trying to be yourself. There are things you might want to be more of. More open, honest, true, authentic or free. Those are all expressions of you. They are not about changing yourself, they are about being yourself. You were enough before, you are enough now and you will continue to be enough as you become more of who you were made to be. Are you feeling unworthy at times? Unworthiness comes from differences you notice by comparing yourself or by some other rejection of loss you have faced. It can also come from a fear you have of not being able to live up to what you really want by projecting yourself forward and anticipating a bad outcome. The problem here is that when you feel unworthy, you automatically make an identity out of your situation. You start to think the unpleasant situation equals yourself, therefore it will always be like this, and you are just not good enough. And there is the problem. You are already perfect on the inside. At the core, we are all equal. Nobody is more worthy than anybody else. Only when you realize that you are already perfect at your core, can you really able to shine out the real you. That moment you will take off the mask you were wearing for far too long. People always want to see the real you; they fall for the authentic true you.

Trust that at your core you are perfect; you just know that there is nothing wrong with you, you are good enough. On the outside you can always improve your skills, but you don't have to identify with them. Start going your way. You will otherwise miss out on being the real you. You not only waste your time at the moment, you will also need some time to forget all the wrong mind-programming about how you should be. Trust your inner self. You don't need evidence or justification to trust yourself. You just do it.

Only then you get the opportunity to let your inner beauty shine through. That way, you are in harmony on the inside and with what you reflect on the outside. Just be. By not thinking about it, you can focus your energies on what is really present in front of you and over time you will feel worthy naturally, by just being you and being present. It can be challenging at times, especially when the society around you differentiates people on superficial levels. Nobody can drag you down without your permission. Nobody has the right to do so. If there is someone who is trying to make you feel unworthy as a human being, just disapprove of that behaviour. You know that at the core you are as worthy as you could be, as anybody could be.

If there is something that you still don't know, just learn from it. If there is something you don't have, it doesn't matter. Your core value is not diminished by that. Coming from the standpoint of equality has a much higher moral value and shows a strong and admirable character. You can be proud of that. In the end, anybody who shows by his actions that he doesn't believe in equality shows a poorness of character.

We all struggle at times with finding our own value. Sometimes we cause self-sabotage and quit things to avoid disappointment. How often do we put everyone else before ourselves? We end up saying yes, when we really want to say no. It can cause silence instead of speaking up when we are upset. It can be the reason we hide behind vices, toxic relationships and crappy jobs. It can be the reason that when no one is looking we feel lost, alone, isolated, stuck and afraid. It has happened to me also, until I realized that if I did not think I was enough, I truly would create a life where I experienced not being enough.

If you desire to feel like you are enough, you have to start by supporting yourself. Start listening to what you say to yourself. Would you give your advice to a small child? Do you say nice things when you look in the mirror? When you try something and fail, do you give yourself credit for trying? When you have a bad day, how do you cope? I started by forgiving myself if I made a mistake and celebrated that I tried. I chose to love myself even when I handled a situation poorly.

When I started to shift my thoughts, I started to see how my life was transforming. Inside I saw love, support and acceptance. That was the moment I found jobs and relationships empowering me. Support is a key ingredient to shift from not feeling like you are enough, but also knowing who you are. Know that you are enough, a beautiful divine creation needed by the world for your unique self and gift. Believe in yourself and all that you are. Embrace change, find your strength and have faith; fall in love with yourself. Start writing feelings down, good and bad. Writing about things is a wonderful way to process them.

You are an incredible person. There is something in you that set you apart from everyone else. You need to find that thing and you need to embrace it, nurture it. As long as you know you are enough, no one can ever tell you that you are not. Being yourself requires far less work and because of that you will be able to invest more time in developing who you are. Find your voice, and change the world. The world wants you to be exactly who you are because nothing will happen if you are not. You are enough and your enough is what changes the world.

Chapter 11: Testimonials

Growing up as a light worker in this timeline has given me great joy to work as a spiritual adviser, a certified angel tarot card reader who was taught by Doreen Virtue and Radleigh Valentine, and to connect with and channel angelic figures and energies to bring guidance and to comfort those around me. I had to go through a growing up and getting to know myself period in life. At times I fell hard and deep, but learned how to put my energies into the right places; chakra healing work took place, and there was a huge amount of psychology to be studied. Mostly I had to understand that all I am is a spiritual being living the human experience.

Over the last several years, I had the pleasure of working with amazing individuals and beautiful souls who live in different countries all over the globe while giving life coaching lessons. Some of them were reading my previous book "Her Whispers - she never left my side", which was published last year in May. Some I shared this book with before the publishing started in order to work on themselves - not only as my clients, but also as new-found friends. I wanted to give what I had inside of me for a long time, and to share that knowledge in order for others to find their path in life. After having several sessions I asked a few of them to   leave some feedback, words   or paragraphs about the book, my work in general, and also the impact it has made on their daily life. I am more than thankful that they have allowed me to put all this together and to be part of "Let it all go". I really do hope and send my prayers out that others will also find completeness and inner healing with this book, as did these friends, clients, and close relatives . There is always something to be thankful for. I received the most beautiful gift someone could get, time. Time is free, but is priceless. You can't own it, but you can use it. You can't keep it, but you can spend it. Once you have lost it, you can never get it back.

Mona Kovacheva, Oslo / Norway

I know Patrick personally and he has always impressed me with his comprehensive and deep intuition about people and events. He has been gifted with strong spiritual sensors, feelings and connecting to invisible energies and the metaphysical world around us. This book is a journey for self-rediscovering, prompting us to ask the core questions of our own purpose and desires in life, which is currently blurred by our fast-paced, digitally saturated lifestyle. With his book, Patrick offers a sanctuary for the mind, a positive pit stop for our own thoughts, guiding them to focus back within us in order to start building a positive emotional core. Every chapter is therapeutic, written in a very welcoming and approachable style, which further encourages the reader to transform into state of personal realization and awareness. Patrick gives insights on how to read and unlock our inner desires and passions, and give them a strong platform to flourish with the power of our thoughts and mind. His book offers a liberating ride, charging us with hope and positive will to find and be the best of who we are. Highly recommended! Thank you Patrick for a generous and inspirational read!

Marta Szychowska, London / England

Patrick, a beautiful soul, his wise words in this book will have a huge impact on others - for sure had on mine, life and soul journey. He is a gifted person and by sharing his story and experience, his gift is showing us the way to live happy, full of love and joy, to find a balanced life. His words are inspiring and giving courage to start living in the moment, enjoying our lives with no regrets or sorrows from the past. He helps forgiving what happened to us and to focus on our desires, living a better life. Every word was healing my soul. I felt wonderful after reading his book, not only the current one but also his previous book: Her Whispers-she never left my side. From both the writings I felt full with faith and strength. It helped me to believe how powerful and strong I am as a person. I found huge potential in myself, therefore Thank you Patrick for your lovely soul here on Earth.

Anna Christina Ojala Scarff, London / England

In this book Patrick has put incredible helpful words describing feelings and thoughts. He has managed to explain true emotions and how we feel from the inside most of times. Patrick guides how to learn to love ourselves and also others. The subject of this book is clear and something so real and important that it can be easily read by anyone of us. The writing is touching and honest. It made myself think about how I feel about myself and who I really am and wanting to be. Acceptance is important. Patrick explains this deep and spot on with words of his own charm. Patrick has given me good guidelines and the book will make all of us look at our own inner beauty and willingness to love and accept each other. It is a guide to find true happiness and to love everyone from within and not to be scared of what is to come when one door is closing. Understanding the difference between wanting and needing. I can see how this book will possibly guide one out of darkness and into a content self, letting go of the dark from within.

Paige Betlem, London / England

Have you ever been drowning? I must have been 15, a sunny day during my summer camp trip to the river I realised with horror that suddenly the sandy bottom of the river was gone and I could not control what was happening. I was calm, I just could do nothing about that situation and I started to go down. My life rushed before my eyes and the next thing I remember was one of the older boys pulling me by the hair to the surface. Fast forward twenty five years. With a great career in hospitality Sales behind me, a loving husband and 3 adorable children later I found myself in a very similar situation. I was drowning. But this time it was a different, scary drowning. I was so exhausted from the everyday, school runs, Library, Children's centre, cleaning, cooking etc. So, from a happy person with a sparkle years ago, I turned out into a Housewife wearing PJ's. I used to shout at my kids, my relationship with them and especially my Dad has deteriorated. I was going to bed every night feeling horrible for the way I became and promised to myself that the next day I would stop. I just could not break this vicious cycle. I was going down the same scenario every day.

I truly believe that having Patrick in my life saved me from drowning into depression and from a big black scary place I was heading head down, like Alice in the rabbit hole. His big heart, his amazing sense of humour but mostly his wisdom and gift as a Spiritual adviser helped me to change things in my life, which I just had no power to change on my own. He guided me every step of the journey, was my soul mate, my team member, my torch in the darkness. I was incredibly lucky to read this book, which opened my eyes and made me realise where I was going wrong and the huge importance of cutting the cords with the past, forgiving and moving forward in piece. Patrick is one of the most positive people you can come across. It is incredible, how such a young person in his 30's can be so wise and almost philosophical. I am so grateful to Patrick for restoring the inner me and making me believe and loving myself again! Things are not perfect yet, as healing is a long and multi-level process, but he is holding my hand and walking with me.I am so eternally grateful to him and I know he will lead other souls to their light, love and harmony as he helped me.

Wim Van Zyl, Cape Town / South Africa

I found myself at a deep dark place in my life, which I chose to sit and stay in for a while. What was my purpose in life? I was gently guided to read Patrick's first book "Her Whispers- she never left my side", mentioning I haven't read any books for a very long time. Patrick's book was pivotal to me in hearing the Whispers of my own ancestors and spiritual guides. A gentle call to see and hear the symbols that surround me every day. Patrick became a light in a transition vase; he guided, shared and gave of himself in a way that was needed and profound. Patrick guided me to hear and see the signs he has experienced from his own Spirit guide, his loving grandmother in my own life. He made me aware of the healing possibility, after the passing of my partner.

The healing with my own grandmother in heaven started happening. Patrick was an obedient voice and guided me to embark on a focused journey with some other Spiritual work. Finally I felt I have found what I have been looking for. I can see the light in me now and it is bright, I feel like a being of light. I am finally embracing what I am radiating. Patrick's willingness to do his work profoundly impacted my life and the course of my road. Thank you very much dear Patrick.

Virve Vaari, Helsinki / Finnland

When meeting Patrick first, I've felt like I've known him my "whole life". When we met, I felt if he belonged to my own family. His extraordinary ability to feel and understand feelings in others without saying any word are simply wonderful. In my mind I call him "My Angel Boy". The words he uses in his this book to express self-awareness, feelings, his own opinions in the identification of feelings and the needs that we all have, is clear, consistent, therapeutic, and helps one realise things in your own personal life, which at that very moment we may not be have realised or understood fully just yet.

Because of this realisation that we go through while reading the book, the future is suddenly easier to see and we find our self-looking at what the future holds in a brighter context, full of opportunities. Thank you, Patrick. By reading this book you have opened my eyes and my mind to see things in a much deeper way. It has been a great therapy. I highly recommend reading "Let it all go" and getting it for your own, so that you may return to it again and again. Love is all that matters.

Cecilia Holmgren, London / England

I feel Patrick's most important chapter of the book is the one about Love. Love is a basic human need, but it's not always as simple as that. Patrick describes perfectly how and why we fall in love and the issues surrounding the love we sometimes crave, even though it may not be what we need. I think we have all been there, in a destructive relationship with someone we thought we loved, but in reality we just depended on them to fill a hole in our lives. Our feelings towards the other person become more like an addiction and it's not the same thing as real love. Patrick also mentions that everything comes from within, as well as the power of our thoughts. This is also extremely important. In my own personal journey, I have learnt exactly that everything is a choice. It's not always easy to choose to be happy or to choose the right path in life, but they are still very much choices. Sometimes it's easier to give in to sadness, loss or anger and that it fine too, as long as we don't let it consume us. I know, Patrick's book could help people understand themselves better and hopefully guide them towards choosing happiness and love.

Bartek Fetysz, London / England

I've met Patrick years ago. I believe in energies of people and places and same attracts always same, believe it or not. My grandmother used to heal people and animals with herbs and prayers, also she reads from tarot cards, same as Patrick does. At the age of 13 I met my Auntie who can read from hands and eyes. She told me I will find out about my special talent in the near future. And so it all began. At the age of 16 I discovered I could read from hands and eyes and I started working with Runes, Scandinavian signs. There we are, a very spiritual past. I never thought when meeting Patrick first, he would be on the same wave of thinking and then he released a book about Angels and his own Spirit Guide who loved him unconditionally and opened doors for him, never imagined. That heavily tattooed guy reading from auras, cards and energies? And here he was. Patrick now released this second book, after the first one that has been very successful. What is so special about him? Only he knows and people who have met him. He did an angel tarot card reading for me, which was on point. Patrick has given me access to this book and I started reading the chapters. It actually hit me hard, he is speaking my mind. Who are we without loving ourselves?

Who are we without not investing in ourselves? Where is our place on this planet? We do not spend enough time these days thinking about ourselves. This book, "Let it all go", like his previous one is making us think, it makes us sit down and wonder. I have spent hours coming back to my roots, to my interests in a specific religion and to my gifts of also reading tarot cards same as Patrick does. After reading just a few chapters of this book, I can tell best is treating it as a meditation. Open it, smell the paper, open it on whatever page and read the sentence your eye gets guided to on this page.

This book was written to awake us. To give us some time for our self. Patrick is sharing something special with all of us. Don't just enjoy it. Let this book lead us into our new journey. The journey to our soul.

Aniko Szalay, London / England

When meeting Patrick first, he completely changed mine and my mother's life with his spiritual work and his calming and healing coaching sessions. Our mind is so powerful as he explains in this book, there is nothing in the world that can stop us believing in our power, as humans we are unique and beautiful and Patrick is one of the most inspiring souls in this world, he certainly added extra value to my life, helped me understand we have to love ourselves and appreciate every little thing we got, I am now getting up in the morning and I am thankful towards the universe for everything I could possible wish for. We got to appreciate also the little things in order to understand life, even if something doesn't go as we want it to be, life goes on and brings you better and bigger when least expected.

Patrick reassured me one day of my inner and outside beauty as a spiritual being living in a human body with a shiny soul, he made me understand that I am unique like all of us are. I am the most important person in my life and I am life. Thank you Patrick, I have a positive mind set now and I am learning who I really am more with every day.

Linda Macintyre, Phoenix Arizona / USA

"Let it all go" provided me with not only the encouragement, but also the specific action steps to take in order to heal my past and live in the present with hope for the future. Patrick offers a fresh and new perspective on an often-discussed topic. I am so grateful to him for writing this helpful guide.

Chapter 12: Thank you

There is still a part of you who wants to give and live. I will always love you more than you could possibly imagine, and your soul will live in mine until the day arrives we can hug each other again. Together as a team, we get green lights wherever we go. Thank you for making my wishes come true and for putting all this together and sending so many beautiful beings into my life to find myself and to become a better version of myself.

You always give a little smile and I give it back to you, because we both know and remember our first encounter. The knowing, I have your back in everything I do gives a satisfied special feeling. You put all of your other duties aside, you leave spotlight out, never set a mark, always there for me, a companion, a guide, a helper, my own protector. We all need leadership and I am just thankful, I have the best one around. You have seen me late at night coming to harm at times, dancing in some devil's arms, really nothing you could have done. Your eyes fiery, unquenched until turned into peace when I started listening to you.

I have always put all my heart pain into yours, accepted unconditional love. Every little thing that ever happened in my life, you have prepared me for what was meant to come. Never wanted me to give up on something I really wanted, the wait a difficult road at times it was, but more painful the regret you taught me. You made me understand clearly a big reason people resist taking chances, because the focus on what they have to give up, rather than what they could gain is too big. When there was something I never had, will need to do something I have never done.

Grandmother, you made me believe that I was truly worth of love, affection, attention, acceptance, worthy of being chosen, worthy of being successful, worthy of succeeding, and to reach for my own dreams. When I own it, you said, I will be able to let it go. Happiness is what you wish for me, to sail away from the safe harbour, catching the trade winds, explore, dream and discover. I will never let you go my Angel. Always yours, "Patrickele ".

Chapter 13: Gita Kurdpoor

"Patrick was sent to me exactly at a moment in my life where I needed to let go of certain aspects. Getting to know him and his comforting words showed me the power of the universe echoing back. It is really like a mirror. What you give or shout out, you get back. Situations you are in, always attracting like minded. Not long before I got introduced to Patrick, I have done a series of pictures, black and white portraits, representing emotions and feelings throughout different stages in my life. Hearing about the different chapters in his book, I knew that all of the pictures taken by myself would fit perfectly with his manuscript. Every chapter he writes about describes a phase I have been in. Patrick's words are not only touching but also awakening my soul, mirrored in the pictures.

Taking a picture, a self portrait is very popular at present and has been since modern technology took over. Those moments captured represent an emotion, felt on a deep level at a specific time. This very special moment won't be given twice, therefore the popularity.

Already before a camera was invented, humans used mirrors to see themselves in this self portrait light. The second we walk away from it, the portrait will fade and with it the memory. The words Patrick has carefully chosen in his book are in balance with the pictures taken. I have trusted my emotions to the camera given at that time. It has given me comfort, hold and a new dimension has opened up for me. The dimension of my very own self capturing. With this collaboration I have learned getting to know myself from within, the honesty found from the pictures and my way back home. I have learned to let it all go".

Since a very young age Gita Kurdpoor has worked as a professional make up artist all over the globe, realised in an early stage she could capture certain details differently to others. With taking pictures of unique, interesting human beings, she has found her love in photography and art. Gita finds emotions throughout her eyes and has a special way to capture them. The moment she captures, she finds comfort in the other persons' soul. She also has a very unique talent to draw feelings into paper with a pencil only. Art is an overflow of emotions into action, as she calls it.

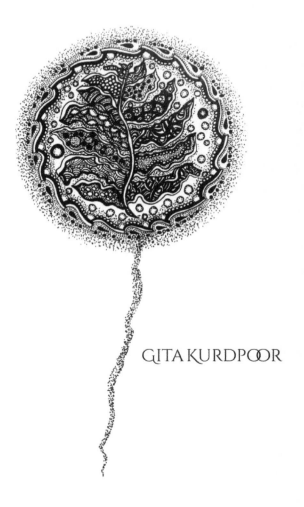

GITA KURDPOOR

Phone : +49 1783124676

Email : gk@gitakurdpoor.com

Website: gitakurdpoor.com

Instagram.com/gitakurdpoor

The best kinds of people are the ones that come into your life and make you feel the sun where you once saw clouds. The people that believe in you so much, you start to believe in you too. The people that love you, simply for being you. The once in a lifetime kind of people. Gita came into my life in the most unexpected time, but my soul just knew, the core of this friendship has a deep bond. I am so proud and thankful for this collaboration. Such a beautiful and loving being.

Patrick x